The Buildings of Georgian Lancaster

A. J. WHITE

Centre for North-West Regional Studies
University of Lancaster

2000

Series Editor: Jean Turnbull

The Buildings of Georgian Lancaster

by Andrew White

This volume is the 39th in a series published by the
Centre for North-West Regional Studies at the
University of Lancaster.

ISSN 0308-4310

First edition 1992;
this revised edition 2000

Published by the Centre for North-West Regional
Studies, University of Lancaster

Designed, typeset and originated by
Carnegie Publishing Ltd, Chatsworth Road, Lancaster
Printed and bound in the UK by
The Cromwell Press, Trowbridge, Wilts

British Library Cataloguing-in-Publication data
A CIP record for this book is available from
the British Library

ISBN 1-86220-084-X

Contents

Acknowledgements

I would like to thank a number of people for their help in putting this book together. My greatest debt of gratitude is to John Champness for advice, information and useful discussions. Jonathan Ratter and Stephen Gardner also lent some of their first-rate first-hand knowledge of the buildings, and the latter also provided a number of building plans. My colleagues Susan Ashworth, Paul Thompson and Wendy Moore respectively read the text and provided graphic and other help. At Lancaster Town Hall John Lee gave me access to deeds and unravelled the complexity of their filing while at Lancaster Central Library Isobel Gaddes and Susan Wilson uncomplainingly found, fetched and carried piles of manuscripts. Finally Katrina Hunter, Sandra Wilkinson and Helen Griffiths typed innumerable versions of my text.

Acknowledgements to second edition

I am still grateful to those who helped with the first edition but would like to add a few more names, especially of those who have let me see their houses or their property deeds. These include June Green and Jenny Betts, Peter Hearne, Vincent Hearne, Holden & Wilson, George Howson, Marsh & Co., Mr J. Parkinson, Mr Penfold, John Regan, Mrs. Denise Robertshaw, Prof. John Sawyer, Steven and Rosemary Watson, Martin Widden, and others too numerous to mention, who I hope will forgive my omission. I would also like to thank staff at the Lancashire Record Office and at Lancaster Central Library, especially Jenny Loveridge. Finally I have been lucky enough to have the run of the splendid series of property deeds in Lancaster Town Hall, referred to in the notes as 'LCC Deeds', one of the best sources of all.

Introduction

The Georgian buildings of Lancaster have not until now received the attention they deserve.

A long vernacular tradition of sturdy building, enhanced by the qualities of Lancaster stone, a short period of prosperity at a time of general good taste and a slump in the nineteenth century have left Lancaster with an exceptional range of houses and public buildings of the eighteenth and early nineteenth centuries. The abiding memory of Lancaster is of a Georgian town.[1] Some 250 buildings of Georgian date survive in the city centre in recognisable form and many others appear in old photographs. The attrition rate of Georgian buildings has not been high because on the whole they have always been of recognised worth, but this did not stop the loss of a few significant buildings in key locations.

Prosperity came with the growth of port trade in the mid-eighteenth century, although a rebuilding boom had started somewhat earlier, changing Lancaster from a town of timber and thatch to one of stone. The establishment of St George's Quay in 1750–55 and the New

'South View of Lancaster', an engraving by Woolnoth after Farington, 1816. To an extent which has been almost forgotten, Lancaster was regarded in the 18th and early 19th century as a picturesque place in its own right, as well as being the natural stopping place for travellers to the Lake District. Its dignified architecture, attractive stone, and views towards Ingleborough and Morecambe Bay contributed to this in no small measure.

Quay in 1767 materially assisted the handling of goods. New warehouses and a splendid Custom House set the seal on trading success, which brought the produce of the West Indies and of the Baltic through the port of Lancaster.[2] The port facilities of Lancaster are a rare survival from the period before fireproofing. The outward and visible sign of general prosperity was the quantity and quality of public and private rebuilding.

Nos 76 (*right*) and 78–80 (*left*) Church Street, town houses respectively of the Marton family and the Wilsons of Dallam Tower. No. 76 is an older house refronted in the 1730s or 1740s and has extensive oak panelling, while nos 78–80 was built in 1772–75 and contains fine mahogany doors.

The trading success coincided with a developing social calendar, hingeing on the Assizes, held twice each year in the Castle, and the Races, held on the Marsh until 1807 and on Lancaster Moor from 1809. The atmosphere of the Assizes in the nineteenth century is admirably conveyed by Thomas de Quincey in his essay 'The English Mail-Coach',[3] where he describes the flood of lawyers and gentry into town on these occasions. Sir George Head, writing in 1835, also gives a flavour of the atmosphere:[4]

The Assizes were unluckily on that very day at their zenith: a festival, of which the signs and phenomena belowstairs, and in the streets, were apparent; – bloated country coachmen, in their best liveries, stood lounging in the stable-yards and gateways; every servant in the house jostled and trod on the heels of his fellow; dinner tables were laid in all the parlours; sand, in preparation for the scuffle, was spread on the floor instead of carpets; the lawyers ran to and fro in their wigs, and a group of hungry farmers in the passage, all panting and eager for the fray, whetted their large teeth, and licked their lips, as they snuffed up the sweet savour, or fragrant odour, from the kitchen ...

This description is almost certainly applicable also to the previous century.

It became fashionable for landed society to entertain during the Assizes and Races, when the theatre was also at its busiest. A number of the minor nobility and gentry built town houses for this purpose. Amongst these were Dr Daniel Wilson of Dallam Tower near Milnthorpe, Mr John Fenton Cawthorne MP of Wyreside Hall, Mr Oliver Marton of Capernwray, and Charles Strickland, whose country house was Sizergh Castle. (He also had a town house in Kendal.)[5] However, most of the large new houses were built for successful merchants, such as the Rawlinsons and Salisburys. Many of these houses, and those of the new occupants of Dalton Square etc., were designed for entertaining, with large public rooms on the ground floor and a private drawing room above.

The prosperity attracted able architects such as Thomas Harrison and J. M. Gandy. For the first time the public purse, in the form of the County or the Corporation, was able to pay for new public buildings, the latter by borrowing, from the sale of investments and from the growing receipts from the sale and lease of land for private building. Their buildings included alterations to the Castle for courts and gaol, Skerton Bridge, the County Lunatic Asylum and the Town Hall.[6]

After 1800 the pace slackened; the wars with France cost a high price in lives, ships and cargoes lost to privateers. By 1820 the prosperity was largely at an end. It saved the inheritance of Georgian architecture because there was little money to rebuild. Not everything survives of course, but Victorian Lancaster was a very different place with different values and aspirations. It was content, in most cases, to subdivide and alter existing buildings rather than to demolish and rebuild. Of course most of the older streets contain some Victorian buildings and the textile mills lining the canal were a new and substantial feature of the town after 1800, leading to a wholly different economy.[7]

There are many reasons for the collapse of prosperity. The movement of merchants to Liverpool, which had a greater range of specialist services such as marine insurance, and the slump following the Napoleonic wars affected Lancaster badly. So did the slackening of trade with the West Indies. However, the failure of the town's two banks within a few years of each other in the 1820s destroyed much of Lancaster's credit and liquidity. It is computed that £420,000 at the prices of the day was lost in the two failures, and that was almost entirely borne by citizens of Lancaster. Some of it was paid back in due course, but the town took a long time to recover.[8]

Investment of savings at that time, before

the coming of the railways, was a very localised activity and the consequences of bank failures were felt most keenly over a very small area. It is unlikely that anyone in Lancaster had much money to spare for building during the 1830s and 1840s and so the new buildings of this period are churches such as St Thomas', the railway stations and the Oddfellows' Hall, all dependent upon the finances of a wider area.

Whatever the causes of Lancaster's economic decline the effect is that there was little money about to rebuild, extend or demolish older buildings after about 1820. As a result we have a very fine legacy of Georgian buildings, including virtually the whole of the eighteenth-century quayside, to enjoy and cherish for the future.

Stone Sources

Lancaster is fortunate in having a variety of building stone, suitable for different purposes, available within a short distance.

For exterior walling flush-jointed ashlar

blocks were readily available. Many specifications called for 'polished freestone' which in effect meant the local sandstone rubbed to a flat finish, leaving no tooling marks. Such

Some examples of stone-dressing using Lancaster stone.
Clockwise: 4 Queen Street, *c.* 1770 ('polished freestone' with lightly feathered borders); 5–7 Queen Street, *c.* 1780 (false rusticated jointing in very large blocks); Shire Hall, *c.* 1790 (punch dressed); Girls' National School, High Street, 1820 (horizontally broached and bordered).

Detail from a oil painting by William Linton of Lancaster from the Moor. This detail shows the quarries still in operation, with very large stone blocks detached and ready for lifting onto a cart with the aid of sheerlegs. Although it dates from about 1870 the techniques are exactly the same as those used by Georgian stone masons. (Lancaster City Museums)

freestone came from Lancaster Moor, especially 'Windmill Hill' or 'Knotts' – there were up to seven separate quarries on the Moor during the eighteenth century. Another source was 'Mr George Gibson's Quarry near the Greaves in Scotforth'.[9] This was near the site of the present Brunton House.

Contemporary descriptions and recently-cleaned buildings suggest that the stone was almost white when fresh. However, where it has not been blackened by smoke the stone has generally weathered to a honey colour, with brownish streaks caused by iron impurities. That these were an original feature of the stone is borne out by the description of an anonymous Nottinghamshire visitor to Lancaster in 1764.[10] Of the new Custom House he says; '... a very handsome new building with a neat portico facing the river supported by four plain pillars,

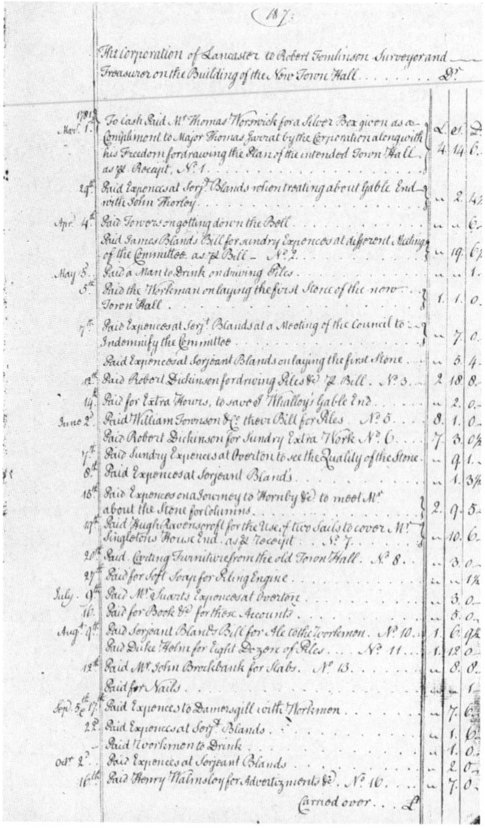

The handwritten ledger reads, in part:

The Corporation of Lancaster to Robert Tomlinson Surveyor and Treasurer on the Building of the New Town Hall

A page from the accounts of Robert Tomlinson in the Bailiffs' Book for the building of the new Town Hall in 1781. It contains three references to the search for suitable stone at Overton (Bazil quarry), Hornby and Damasgill (Ellel).

each formed of a single stone, beautifully veined ...'

Benjamin Newton, Rector of Wath, described this stone in 1818: 'The blocks of stone that were lying at the Castle to build a new tower were some of the finest I ever saw and Lancaster is greatly indebted for its appearance to the Stone with which it is built ...'[11] It is likely that those buildings which were of rubble stonework rather than ashlar were faced with render of some sort. Some evidence comes from door and window mouldings, which are often rebated as though to frame expanses of render. Further support comes from the American Quaker Jabez Maud

Fisher, who came here in 1775. He noted: '... the houses of Stone either hewn [i.e. ashlar] or rough Cast ...'[12] The Moor quarries and that at Scotforth now show no exposed faces. The latter has been largely built over, while the former quarry rights on the Moor were bought out and the area landscaped in the 1870s and 1880s to form Williamson Park.

These freestone sources belong to the Namurian gritstone series. Another source, where exposed faces can still be seen, was at Damasgill or Mainstones Quarry in Ellel, seven miles south of Lancaster. The particular benefits of this stone seem to have been that it could be worked in very large blocks and that it had good water-resisting qualities. It was used for the monolithic columns of the Custom House in 1762–63, possibly for the columns of the Assembly Room (after 1759) and for the massive sections of the columns of the Old Town Hall of 1782–83. At Glasson Dock it was specified for the dock walls by the Port Commissioners in 1787.[13]

A description of 1820[14] characterises the stone thus: '... being of a peculiar nature not subject to decay, of a coarse but solid texture, free from those deceitful seams which too much of this country freestone abounds with.'

The fells east of Lancaster also provided two other useful types of building stone. For the fire-places and parts of the flooring of the Custom House Richard Gillow specified 'Haw-Clough' or 'Clougha' flags.[15] Clougha, a prominent outlier of the Bowland fells, was the nearest source of fissile sandstone and different quarries produced different thicknesses and qualities.[16]

Thinner sandstone flags had been used for roofing since Roman times, and in the local vernacular of the seventeenth century a whole range of sizes were used; very large at the eaves and progressively smaller towards the ridge. By the mid-eighteenth century, however, Lake District slate was becoming available. For the Custom House Richard Gillow specified; 'the Second Sort of Coney-Stone Slate equally as

Gardyner's Chantry in St Marygate. This group of almshouses was originally founded in the fifteenth century and, unusually, survived the Reformation. In 1792 it was rebuilt as four houses at the same time as the large house immediately to the east, and detailed building accounts survive, rare for modest structures.

good, as that upon Captn. Henry Fell's new House at Fleet Bridge'.[17] By the end of the century the use of Coniston slate was commonplace in the town. It allowed much lighter roof structures and shallower pitch to the roofs. Despite this there were still some thatched buildings in the town as late as 1810.

The tradition of stone guttering, a feature of the seventeenth century, was coming to an end. On most Georgian buildings in Lancaster lead flashing and lead-lined guttering with downspouts cast or rolled out of lead were becoming commonplace. Lead of various weights per foot is carefully prescribed for various functions in contemporary building specifications, such as that for the Town Hall in 1781, where lead of not less than eight pounds per square foot is specified for the pediment.[18] Presumably the growth in the use of lead reflects its greater availability by sea, via the port.

Because of the ready access to good stone Lancaster had no need for much brick building. Indeed a description of Lancaster in 1825[19] declared that the town had then only one such building. This was probably the Poorhouse in Wyresdale Road, a building of 1787–88, now gone. Brick was, however, used extensively where it was not seen. The arches under the portico of the Custom House, for instance, were turned in brick, presumably for greater ease and lower cost. The rear wing of nos 1–3 Cable Street is also in brick, a very rare example of its external use in Lancaster, dating from 1759. Richard Gillow, with his London training, probably had no personal prejudice against the use of brick but was prepared to acknowledge the local desire for facing in stone.

During the restoration of the Custom House in 1983–84 it was found that away from the front elevation many of the walls were effectively of timber box construction, infilled with brick and faced in stone rubble. The use of structural timber to tie and stiffen walls even in quite sophisticated Georgian buildings has been noted elsewhere.[20] In Lancaster it can be found in lintels over doors and windows and as bressumers buried within the stonework. Much old roofing timber was probably recycled in this way. In the Sun Inn, Church Street, no. 11 Chapel Street and several buildings in New Street and Market Street, the use of timber framing infilled with laths or wattle for most internal walls should alert us to how common the practice was.

Useful building accounts survive for the Custom House, Town Hall and Assembly Room.[21] Among lesser buildings we have some useful accounts for the rebuilding of Gardyner's Chantry as four small cottages in 1792.[22] Unfortunately all too little is known about private houses. We do, however, know

1 and 3 Cable Street, photographed in the 1920s when the railings to the front were complete and before the left-hand half was unceremoniously beheaded. What makes this act of vandalism even more sad is that this pair of houses (of the late 1750s) is one of the very few that can be certainly attributed to Richard Gillow, architect and cabinetmaker.

Lancaster Castle in 1778, from a drawing by Thomas Hearne, on the eve of the rebuilding which was later to transform it. Virtually everything visible in this view is of medieval origin, apart from the rather weak curtain walls which replaced those demolished at the end of the Civil War.

that experience from Capt. Fell's house, then recently built, was incorporated into the Custom House, so it is likely that much the same procedures and specifications were used. By today's standards these specifications were ridiculously brief and allowed of differing interpretation. Of course many of the masons were working in a long tradition and needed only a front elevation or details of windows and doors to produce a respectable building. Argument sometimes sprang from the vagueness of the brief and could lead the architect and the builder into conflict with the client; this occurred at both Glasson Dock and at St George's Quay, where both clients and masons were unfamiliar with the work.

The rear of the Castle in 1778, before work began on the improvements. From a watercolour drawing by Thomas Hearne. (Lancaster City Museums)

Architects

Many of Lancaster's Georgian buildings were not formally designed by architects at all but were, in the fashion of the time, put up by master masons working from pattern books. Practical solutions, born out of long experience, were found to problems which arose in construction. Even where there was an architect matters of constructional detail were often left for the mason to sort out and the architect often drew just the main elevations. Usually the mason acted as foreman and clerk of works all in one.

Architects found themselves increasingly in demand, however, and particularly for public buildings. Lancaster was fortunate in having the services of two men, Richard Gillow and Thomas Harrison, who were architects of a very high standard. Other names of the period were Major Thomas Jarrett, Henry Sephton, and Joseph Gandy. The architect and builder

of the Aqueduct Bridge, Alexander Stevens, is also worthy of mention. This was his last and finest work – he died in 1796 before it was completed – and possibly the finest piece of canal architecture in the country.[23] His monument can be seen on the south wall of the Priory church. Apparently his son, of the same name, carried on working as an architect in Lancaster for many years after and it is surprising that we can not identify a single building which he may have designed.

Richard Gillow, born in 1734, was the son of Robert Gillow, founder of the well-known Lancaster cabinet-making firm. He was trained in London by William Jones, a minor architect. Gillow's training in architecture may have been aimed at helping the firm move into lucrative interior design as well as furniture. At all events Richard did not have much time for his architectural practice because the

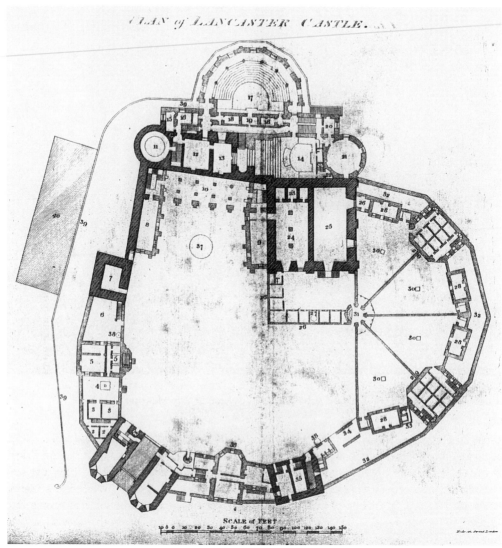

SCALE of FEET

Plan of Lancaster Castle showing the alternations carried out up to 1807, from Clark's *History*. These include the Shire Hall and Crown Court, together with the new gaol buildings to the north. Later work included the Female Penitentiary to the south, replacing the old Dungeon Tower.

cabinet-making business was doing so well. A number of buildings may be ascribed to Gillow, including the Custom House, nos 1 and 3 Cable Street, no. 1 Queen Square, and possibly also the Catholic chapel in Dalton Square (now Palatine Hall). (The Gillow family were Roman Catholics.) The new Shambles was another important commission of the 1760s, but nothing survives of it. Undoubtedly there

were several others.[24] The Assembly Room has been put forward as Gillow's work, and it is very probable that the musicians' gallery inside is a product of his firm.

Thomas Harrison came to Lancaster in 1783 from Richmond, Yorkshire, after winning the competition to design Skerton Bridge. During the next ten years he made himself indispensible to the Corporation and was called in to

Lancaster Castle showing the Shire Hall from the west, by Robert Freebairn. One of a series of watercolour drawings of work at the Castle, dated 1801. (Lancaster City Museums)

draw up a number of plans and layouts. His Lancaster buildings include Skerton Bridge, the tower of St John's church, added in 1784, the cupola of the Old Town Hall, an alteration of 1783 from Jarrett's original plan (*q.v.*), and Quernmore Park Hall, three miles to the north east. His principal work was, however, upon Lancaster Castle where he started in 1788 upon the Governor's House, and left, after many recriminations, in 1799, his work still incomplete. During this period and again up to *c.* 1823 the medieval castle was transformed into a modern prison with new courts etc.

Harrison was latterly working on both Lancaster and Chester castles, where he can be seen respectively in Gothick and Grecian mood. He did not live in Lancaster after 1793.[25] His work on Lancaster Castle was continued by Joseph Gandy.

Henry Sephton is known for only one building in Lancaster. Sephton, a Liverpool man, designed the new tower for the Priory church between 1753 and 1755, after the collapse of its predecessor.[26] While it has one or two contemporary features it is otherwise very much in the revived 'Gothick' style, a very early example. It has a mixture of styles – a Chinese chippendale fret on the transom, a chubby Georgian angel above the louvres, and Gothic crockets. He may also have been responsible for St John's church, one commission perhaps leading to another.

Major Thomas Jarrett, architect of the old Town Hall, was an Irish military engineer. He appears in the Army List as 'Engineer Captain in Ireland' since 1766 and Major since 1780, and must have come to England very shortly before his work at Lancaster, perhaps still as a serving officer, which would explain the lack of payment.[27] The somewhat massive and old-fashioned building would suit very well an architect more accustomed to barracks and military works. Since the Genealogical Office in Dublin Castle was designed *c.* 1760 by a Joseph Jarrett[28] there may well be a family connection. Joseph is also recognised as the architect of St Catherine's church in Dublin, which bears similarities to the Town Hall.[29]

Edward Batty is another architect of whom we know very little. There is no single building with which he can now be associated, but his name appears on a handbill in connection with the sale of land by the Dalton estates in 1783. He was subsequently responsible for the layout of Dalton Square and its associated streets in the same year, if not for the design of specific buildings.[30] Plots of land were sold off and individuals had their own houses built, but to a carefully specified standard of height and finish.

When traces of the Dominican Friary were found in the construction of Sulyard Street, it was Batty who measured and described the remains. He died 22nd February 1807 aged 67 and is buried at St John's. His tombstone, which describes him as 'Architect', can be seen at the south-east corner of the church. Other sources, however, record Batty as a joiner and cabinet-maker living in Chapel Street in 1794–96,[31] so 'Architect' is perhaps a title to which he aspired, while spending most of his working life as a surveyor and carpenter.

Another shadowy figure is that of William Coulthart, who practised during the 1820s and 1830s in both Greek Revival and Gothic style. His work is known at Halton, at the Hall and the Rectory, and he carried out designs for a new vestry at the Priory church in 1827. He also seems to have designed the Savings Bank (present Children's Library) and the Amicable Society Library building now occupied by the Royal Bank of Scotland. A Trade Directory of 1834 records the address of his Lancaster office as Castle Grove. More research needs to be carried out to establish his oeuvre.[32]

Thomas Standen, architect of the County Lunatic Asylum, was a slater and plasterer by background, and had worked as such on the Roman Catholic chapel (he was a Catholic). He later went bankrupt and moved to Liverpool. Standen gave detailed evidence at the Tatham v. Wright Will Cause in 1834 about work he had tendered for at Hornby, unsuccessfully it would seem. No other buildings by him are at present known.[33]

Masons and Craftsmen

It has already been remarked that in many building projects the roles of mason and architect had not yet been fully separated.

Some of the early mason/architects have left no documentary trace, but we know of two from the late 1670s because they worked on the harbour at Whitehaven.[34] Richard Caton and Roger Lawson were Lancaster masons called in to solve problems in building the piers there. Perhaps they had gained experience from building quays on Green Ayre for various merchants, or from building bridges in Lunesdale. At all events Richard was drowned in 1680 and Roger left the works.

While they date from before the period of our study it is clear that Lancaster had a rebuilding boom in the late seventeenth and early eighteenth centuries. Men such as these had expertise and were in considerable demand. We know from the autobiography of William Stout that in 1739:

> There being many new buildings erected in the town this year, the masons and wrights were so fully imployed that it prolonged the time in finishing it [sc. Stout's new house].[35]

The successful tenderer for the Custom

House in 1762 was the mason Richard Fisher. He, with Robert Clarkson, slater and plasterer, and William Sharp, plumber, was left to interpret the plan and the very brief details given by Richard Gillow, and to turn them into the building we see today. Some of this team had already worked together on St George's Quay and on the Assembly Room a few years earlier. At the latter building Bryan Clarke, William Kirkby and Richard Fisher had been the masons. Fisher seems to have been the junior at that time but between 1759 and 1762 his stock had risen. He had obtained his freedom in 1753–54, while his older partners had been made freeman in 1739–40 and 1738–39 respectively. He died in 1785 while working on the pier at Glasson. In 1796 his heirs held four houses (built by him?) in St Leonardgate and one in Penny Street.[36]

Robert Fox worked as carpenter at the Assembly Room and on two other houses built for the trustees of William Penny in 1757. He died before he could be paid, but his widow eventually received the money owing. Other names occurring in the building accounts are Stephen Wildman, glazier, John Christopherson, plasterer, James Warriner, glazier and plumber and John Roper, smith (no doubt he supplied hinges, locks, nails etc.)

In the work on the two houses mentioned earlier the carpenter was paid £58 and Robert Bennison and William Crook, masons, only just over £19. This suggests that these buildings were still essentially timber-framed. In such cases the carpenter would no doubt have acted as site foreman over the minor trades represented, while a mason would occupy this role in a mainly stone building.

The grouping of several masons to undertake work was probably a result of payment only being made after the whole job was finished. A single mason might well encounter problems of cash-flow, while several together could spread the burden and find guarantors for their debts, or for the bond they had to enter into, in order to guarantee completion of the work. The successful tenderers for the Town Hall in 1781, Robert Charnley, mason, and Robert Dickinson, carpenter, had to enter a bond of £3,000 before starting work.[37] Charnley was working at nearby Glasson on the new pier in 1781 when he made the contract. There are very full building accounts for the old Town Hall among the Corporation Records.[38]

The contract to build the important and expensive new bridge, now known as Skerton Bridge, between 1782 and 1788, was signed by five masons of the Muschamp family, along with two others. Several of the Muschamps were from Otley, in Yorkshire.[39] Their joint venture may indicate a pooling of family resources to find the costs of materials and tide them over the period until repayment. It is not known whether the same masons built the Bridge Houses, the complex at the south end of the bridge which included the toll-house. Thomas Harrison was certainly the architect of both bridge and houses.

Christopher Clark tells us[40] that in the very considerable rebuilding works at the Castle up to 1807 the superintending mason was Alexander Hayes while the principal carpenter was Edward Exley. Exley had worked with Harrison on the New Bridge, while Joseph Muschamp, one of the masons employed on that project, appears as a supplier of stone 'for the Works at Lancaster Castle' in 1791. Clearly Harrison established a group of craftsmen with whom he could work and took them with him to fresh projects. Much further work is required to establish which other craftsmen were working on the Castle in the late eighteenth and early nineteenth centuries. It is clear that the project offered very substantial contracts and employed many men. From the Corporation records it is clear that a number of the known masons were also leasing quarries on Lancaster Moor, so that they controlled the whole process from quarrying to setting stones. Lists of the lessees of the quarries

St Nicholas Street Chapel, built by the Presbyterians in 1786 and demolished in 1967 to make way for a new shopping development. It is surprisingly sophisticated compared with many other Georgian nonconformist chapels. The architect was a Mr Hurd.

survive for 1752 and 1756[41] and a plan of the quarries for 1814.[42]

A more detailed examination of Lancaster's Georgian masons appears in *The Local Historian*.[43]

Style and Design

From the beginning of the eighteenth century new ideas began to filter into Lancaster. The process took a long time; builders still used traditional methods and the vernacular style common in the seventeenth century continued in use in many smaller buildings. What began to be used more frequently, particularly for larger buildings, was Classical detail and Classical symmetry, derived from study of the ruins of Rome, the writings of the Roman architect and engineer Vitruvius, and the work of Italian architects of the Renaissance.[44]

To start with most influence came from the latter source, at second hand from the works of Palladio, Serlio and others. Gradually English architects became aware of other and older

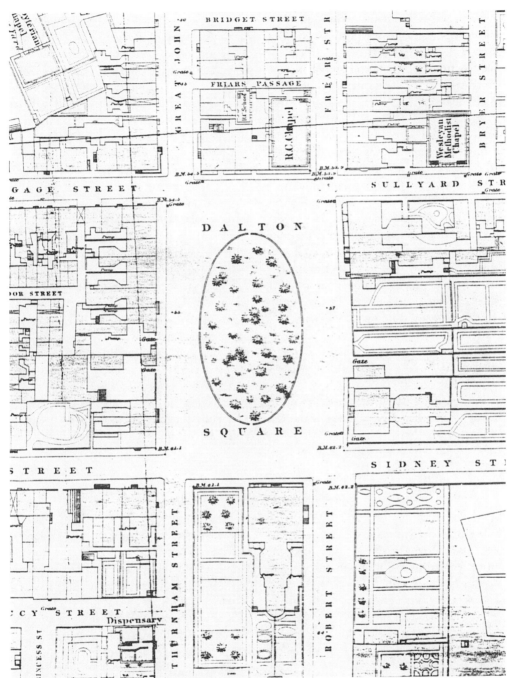

Detail from the 60′ Ordnance Survey map of 1849 showing houses around Dalton Square. Many of them have a type of rear service wing which seems to be distinctive to Lancaster, with a narrowing of the wing and a canted section allowing light to the rear rooms of the main block and in particular to the long stair window at the junction. The canted or chamfered section is often of ashlar, compared with the coursed rubble of the service wing, because it could be seen from the main rooms. (*With the sanction of the Director General, Ordnance Survey*)

An interior view of the Music Room, prior to restoration. The fine plasterwork is thought to be by Italian craftsmen, some of whom are known to have been working in Lancashire in the early 18th century at Burrow Hall and Towneley Hall.

at no. 12 Castle Park in 1819 [57] and the garden wall of no. 5 Dalton Square, now demarcating a car park, is unusually formed of brick with stone 'throughs' at intervals, suggesting that it may have been hollow and heated for espaliered fruit trees. Greenhouses are frequently mentioned, eg. at no. 12 Castle Park and at no. 10–11 Dalton Square in 1793 [58] and these may indicate a more professional approach to gardening in the town. Few of the gardens are large enough to have merited full-time employees, but may have provided work for some of the free-lance gardeners who are listed in the Freedom or Stallenge Rolls.

One or two gardens were more elaborate than usual. The house of the Sherburne family of Stonyhurst in St Nicholas Street had a notable mulberry tree in its garden. [59] Another mulberry tree stood in the garden behind no. 49 King Street, forming a central feature, [60] and a venerable mulberry survives at no. 8 Castle Park. Behind the Sun Inn was a detached garden belonging to the Marton family whose house was no. 76 Church Street. It contained both a planted area and a very ornate summer house, now known as the Music Room, although it seems only to have gained this name in the nineteenth century. [61]

Another summer house stands at the end of the long garden of Greycourt in Church Street. One stood here in about 1724 at the time of William Stukeley's visit [62] but the present octagonal structure probably belongs to the 1770s. A summer-house stood in the garden of no. 1 Queen Square, for instance,

This octagonal summer house stands at the northern end of the garden of Greycourt, 102 Church Street, and enjoys an outlook over the Vicarage Fields, open glebe land since the Middle Ages.

judging from Mackreth's map. Bearing in mind the number of summer houses which have been identified in Kendal as a result of detailed survey work it seems likely that many former summer houses remain to be found on the ground or from maps in Lancaster as well.[63]

Poorer Houses

Where did the poorer people live in Georgian Lancaster? The answer is not straightforward because the evidence is scarce. From various sorts of evidence the answer seems to be that some people lived in those older houses which had not been replaced; in particular in areas like Lower Church Street, Moor Lane and Stonewell, where houses with thatched roofs are depicted by the artist Gideon Yates as late as the early nineteenth century.[64] Others lived in cottages in yards and courts contrived behind houses on the main streets. The process of turning these into slums was well under way by the mid-nineteenth century but from dates on houses such as 1713 in Little John Street, 1714 in Simpson's Yard or 1741 in Golden Ball Yard[65] it is clear that the infilling of former gardens was established surprisingly early. Finally poor people were scattered throughout the town and though there were fashionable areas there were few 'ghettoes' – in fact well-to-do and poor must frequently have lived side by side. This is evident from the Window Tax Returns of 1766,[66] which show a fairly random distribution of names marked 'P' for poor.

The town had a large proportion of transients such as mariners who had no regular dwelling and few possessions. It is probable that they took a room or two in a shared house. Unmarried men often took the same course, however wealthy they were – 'housekeeping' was regarded as something for married men. William Stout's autobiography shows him taking rooms in this way.[67] Widows or older spinsters might occupy rooms including the kitchen and eke out a living providing food for other lodgers, though it was quite common for men in lodgings to eat at public houses, or have food sent in. For many people life as a servant or as an apprentice or journeyman implied living in the master's house and being on constant call, particularly in shops or small businesses. Expectations of privacy were not high in the Georgian period and many poorer people shared rooms or beds or slept under counters.

Where did the money come from?

Lancaster began the eighteenth century with numerous small tradesmen and shopkeepers. By the end of the century many of these people or their successors were calling themselves 'merchants' and had much broader horizons. The merchandise which they dealt with was principally from the West Indies or the Baltic and many dealt in commodities. From the middle of the century, however, Lancaster was heavily involved in the infamous slave trade, collecting slaves from Africa and selling them in the West Indies. This subject is dealt with very well elsewhere,[68] but Charles Dickens well-known passage from the 'Lazy Tour of Two Idle Apprentices' sums up the attitude of Post-Abolition times to the trade and its monuments:

> Mr. Goodchild concedes Lancaster to be a pleasant place, a place dropped in the middle of a charming landscape, a place with a fine ancient fragment of a castle, a place of lovely walks, a place possessing staid old houses richly fitted with old Honduras mahogany, which has grown so dark with time that it seems to have got something of a retrospective mirror quality into itself, and to show the visitor, in the depth of its grain, through all its polish, the hue of the wretched slaves who groaned long ago under old Lancaster merchants ...[69]

Slaving as a business had waned by the end of the eighteenth century in Lancaster, but large fortunes had been made from it. Furniture-making, sugar-refining, soap-boiling, candle-making, sailcloth-weaving and many other legitimate trades helped to secure many a fortune in the town, while professions such as the law or medicine also laid the foundations for many a family's rise to prominence. In the nineteenth century inherited wealth played a large part in the economics of the town, but the eighteenth century had been a time of getting rather than spending.

New Developments

While many of Lancaster's eighteenth-century buildings occupied old sites in the principal streets a series of new developments occurred which took houses outside the previous built-up areas.

The first of these, carried out in a more or less haphazard fashion, was the development of the Green Ayre. The Green Ayre was a crescent-shaped area of land lying between the river Lune and the mill-stream, the latter's course marked today by the line of Damside Street. Originally this had been an area of open space, where citizens took the air in an evening and young people disported themselves.[70] Spillage of buildings on to this space began with the establishment of a series of private quays and warehouses for merchants in the late seventeenth century.[71] St John's church, built in 1754, marks a late stage in this phase, for the church was put there to serve the new population. Further development took place on another part of the Green Ayre later in the century, as we shall see. Although the southern part of the area became a slum in the nineteenth century a number of good houses can still be seen, particularly in Chapel Street.

The next developments, and certainly the first to a coherent plan, were those of St George's Quay (begun 1750), New Street (c. 1745) and New Road (1752). It had been the intention to call New Street 'Charles

Street', but this was reconsidered after the Jacobite rising of 1745 rendered the name politically unsuitable.[72] New Street and New Road were designed to link Market Street with Church Street and Damside Street and were cut through between the medieval burgage plots. New Street retains many of its eighteenth-century buildings on its western side, of which several are converted warehouses. New Road shows little of its eighteenth-century ancestry but an interesting relic found here in 1990 during road works was the old 'sough' or stone-lined drain running down the centre of the roadway, presumably much as it was put in, in 1752.

St George's Quay developed after an Act of Parliament of 1749 enabled the new Port Commission to go ahead with building its legal quays and associated warehouses.[73] A strip of land bordering the river, called 'the Summer Pasture', was obtained on a two-hundred year lease from the Vicar, whose glebe-land it was, and a retaining wall erected along the foreshore. Against this was piled soil and stones, forming a level quay. In 1751, 1753, 1756, and again in 1781 building land was let out in lots, numbered up to 104 and running almost as far as the Pothouse, the delft-ware manufactory.[74] Little control was exercised over what was built and a mixture of private houses, inns and warehouses, of varying character, resulted. Three lots were reserved for the building of a Custom House at the centre of the Quay. This was added in 1764, from

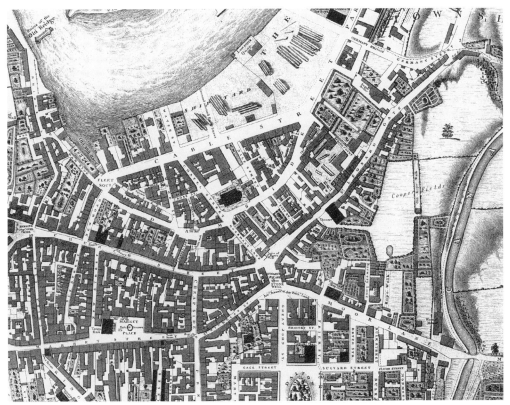

Part of Jonathan Binns' map of Lancaster of 1821, showing the north-eastern part of the town, including the Green Ayre, the crescentic area to the top left of the map. This former island between the millstream and the river was one of the first to be developed, beginning in the late seventeenth century with a series of private quays. Cable Street was laid out with the view to becoming an impressive boulevard giving access to the town from the new bridge further upstream.

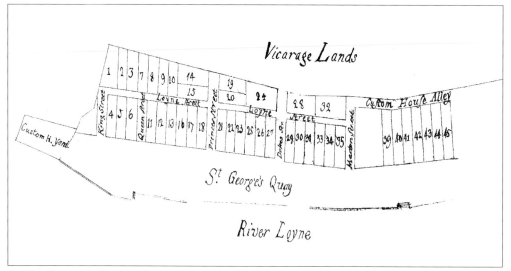

Building lots on St George's Quay in 1754, reproduced from a sale plan among the Port Commission papers. Later on further building lots were let out to the west (the right on this plan). A triple size lot adjacent to lot 39 became the site of the Custom House in 1764, replacing the former Custom House further to the east. The whole development took place on former glebe land.

earlier designs by Richard Gillow. St George has never been particularly associated with Lancaster, so the naming of the quay is probably to be interpreted as a compliment to the reigning monarch, especially in the aftermath of the 1745 rebellion. Demand ran out before supply and the western end of the Quay saw no building, at least until much later.

The warehouses are of a distinctive type of between three and five storeys. Large loading doors for each floor are flanked by windows. At the top a wooden or metal derrick, or a fixed hoist, provided the means of lifting goods from carts on the quay up to the main floors. There was no fireproofing, all the floors being of timber. Access from floor to floor was by a timber staircase in one front corner; most of these staircases have been removed in conversion. In between and behind many of the warehouses were merchants' counting-houses. Most of these have gone or been converted into houses. The whole area represents a most unusual survival of an eighteenth-century port facility without any later overlay.

After a long decline, caused by the failure of the trade for which it was built, this delightful riverside area has undergone a renaissance, many of the warehouses being converted into flats.

Green Ayre saw a scheme for further development in 1784, when a plan was drawn up on behalf of the Corporation showing building lots for sale.[75] The new plan was associated with the building of Skerton Bridge, which was intended to provide a new and better approach to the town from the north. At the Lancaster end of the bridge was to be Bridge Square, with a toll house forming one side. This, now known as the Bridge Houses, was the only building to be completed.[76]

Lining Parliament and Cable Street were to stand smart gentlemen's houses, not less than three storeys high. Other streets with names such as Barbadoes, Jamaica and Antigua Street, recalling Lancaster's trading connections with the West Indies, were to give access to the river bank. On the corner of Jamaica Street a triangular plot was reserved for a public building. Nothing of this was ever built. Clark's

The Custom House, finished in 1764 and designed by Richard Gillow. Its front face is ashlar; its east side coursed rubble; its rear rendered; and its west face originally abutted other pre-existing buildings so was built 'overhand'. Such a prestige building saved most of its impact for the most visible face.

map of 1807 shows buildings only as far east as Water Street, an impression confirmed by J. C. Ibbetson's oil-painting of Cable Street in 1798.[77] It seems that an additional quay was intended to be built here, when the Old Bridge and associated hazards were removed.

The Corporation's aspirations were given a rude shock by a letter from Mr William Bradshaw of Halton, who owned fishery rights in the Lune and much else besides. He claimed that the proposed development breached his rights on the river bank, and threatened to sue. In turn the Corporation hastened to reassure potential buyers that it would defend their right to buy, in court if necessary. There can be little doubt that despite these assurances buyers were confused and put off. The threats effectively destroyed the development.[78]

In 1783 a handbill announced the sale of building lots in the Fryerage. This, the former site of the Dominican Friary, owned by the Catholic Dalton family who lived at Thurnham Hall, had obstructed the eastward development of Lancaster until now. John Dalton obtained a private Act of Parliament in 1784 to break the entail on his estate.[79]

The new scheme, with plans drawn up by Edward Batty, was intended to create a large London-type square with several elegant streets leading off. Building subsequently took place over a period of years, creating the present Dalton Square. Houses were individually designed and built, but had to conform to a standard of height, elevation, and finish; '... each House shall be carried not less than three stories high above the Surface of the Ground ...'[80]

29

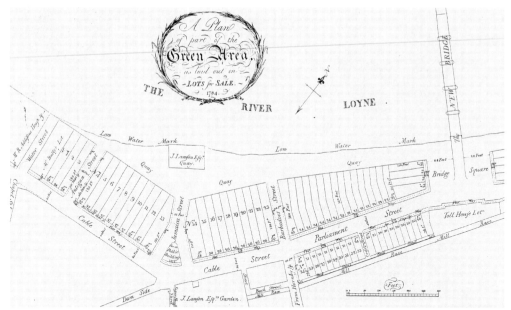

Plan of Green Ayre, marked out in building lots, 1784. Lancaster Corporation was intending to capitalise on some of its spare land and at the same time to make an elegant approach to the town via Bridge Square, Parliament Street and Cable Street. The project never came off, the site later being taken for the Green Ayre station of the Little North Western Railway. (Lancaster City Museums, LM28.25/2)

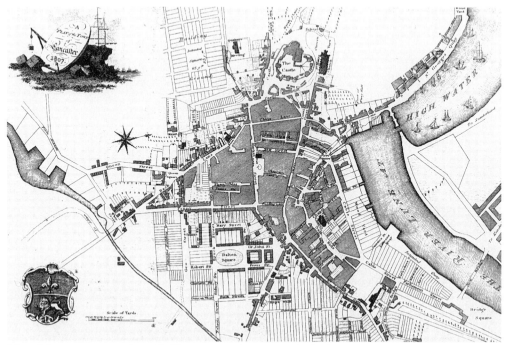

Map of Lancaster in 1807 from Clark's *History*. It shows very clearly the extent of intended development, especially to the east and west. Development eventually took place here, but not in the manner intended. Mid-Victorian working-class housing of a higher density was to occupy much of the open area.

LANCASTER FRYERAGE.

TO BE SOLD,

On Friday *the* 3d *Day of* October, 1783, *at the* Houſe *of Mr.* Thomas Slater, *in the* Fryerage, *in Lancaſter,*

The Sale to begin at 7 o'Clock in the Evening,

On LEASES renewable for ever ;

Subjeſt to ſuch apportioned Ground Rent and other Terms and Conditions as will be produced at the Time & Place of Sale.

DIVERS LOTS OF

BUILDING GROUND,

In the FRYERAGE in LANCASTER,

Divided into a SQUARE and STREETS,

Agreeable to P L A N S prepared ;

AND WHICH

For Public Inſpeſtion will be exhibited in the MER-CHANTS' COFFEE-ROOM, the FRYERAGE HOUSE, at the OFFICE of *Mr. Barrow,* Attorney, and by *Mr. Edward Batty,* Architeſt, all in *Lancaſter* aforeſaid.

✤✤✤✤✤✤✤ LANCASTER : Printed by H. WALMSLEY, Market-ſtreet. ✤✤✤✤✤✤✤

Handbill for the sale of building lots in the Fryerage, 1783. This was to be the site of Dalton Square. Edward Batty drew out the initial plan but the detailed design of houses was the responsibility of individual owners, within some general guidelines. (Lancaster City Museums, LM 74. 121)

An engraving of 1807 after J. C. Ibbetson's 1798 painting of Lancaster from Cable Street. The smart new houses vie for attention with the town's rural and industrial aspects, marked by the cattle and the shipyard in the foreground. No. 1 Water Street is in the centre of the picture.

The west side of Great John Street, looking north, prior to the building of the St Nicholas Centre in 1967. These modest Georgian buildings, their ground floors taken over by shops, formed the northern fringe of the Dalton Square development. All were demolished in 1967.

The names of members of the Dalton family are enshrined in the street names – Great John Street, Mary Street, Bridget Street, and Gage Street, for instance. Access was gained to the new development from Penny Street by demolishing a house belonging to Mr Brockholes; for short the new street was called Brock Street. Another access was via Ffrances Passage, named after the France family of Rawcliffe, who owned the land on which it was built.

Most of the building lots in the new square were let out on forty-one year leases. The lessees were to build a pavement in front and might have cellar entrances not exceeding five feet in front, with railings or 'palisadoes'. Only houses, or a church, were to front the square, and nothing was to be built within the central oval without the approval of two-thirds of the owners.[81]

It appears that a number of the lots were acquired initially by speculators, and fairly quickly sold on. It was the second lessees of each lot who seem to have actually built the houses, or lived there. Lots 17 and 18, for instance, on the west side of the square, were let initially to John Brockbank and Luke Tyson. Christopher Bland, cooper, had acquired lot 18 by 1786 and lot 17 before 1793, when he had built houses on both and sold them to Robert Speight.[82] On the southern side lots 32 and 33 had been let by 1791 to John Shaw, who built the pair of houses which formerly stood there, and he sold them in turn to Thomas Hinde and John Bond respectively.[83]

Many of the houses were sub-let to tenants while a number of those on the western side of the square have lesser houses of broadly the same period built on the rear of their plots, such as those on Gage Street and Mary Street.

Despite the best intentions Dalton Square was never completed as planned, conceived as it was very late in Lancaster's age of prosperity. There are still a number of gaps, or inferior buildings, in Dalton Square and its environs. The lots proved to be too large for Lancaster aspirations, and many were subdivided to create building plots of more manageable size.[84]

Queen's Square (actually a triangle) attempted to give some grace to the southern approach to the town. In its original form it was much more enclosed than it is today; King Street was then a much narrower roadway and the great house of Mr Bowes (now Falcon House) stuck out into it, only being cut back in the 1930s. Queen Street itself began to develop in the last quarter of the eighteenth century. It was not a planned development, but the houses were on virgin sites. Clark's map of 1807 shows further proposed building grounds and an intended square to the west

Dalton Square, looking north in about 1907. Work has already begun on clearing the 'Oval' or garden in the centre for the new monument to Queen Victoria, but the eighteenth-century railings have not yet been replaced by stone balustrading. The absence of traffic gives the square more coherence than it currently enjoys. On the right is the original Roman Catholic chapel of 1798, by now superseded by St Peter's Cathedral in East Road.

Nos 10 and 11 Dalton Square, two of the grandest houses in Lancaster, were replaced by the new Town Hall in 1909. Built in 1791–94 by John Shaw and immediately sold on to Thomas Bond and John Hinde, these houses occupied four building plots and their gardens in Robert Street occupied several more.

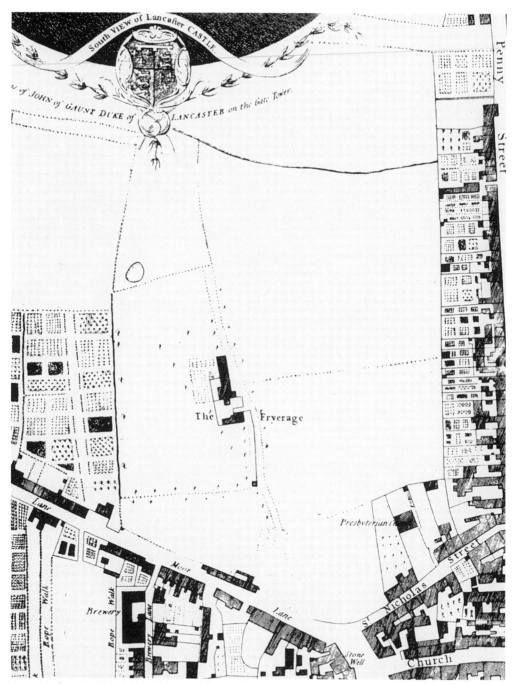

A section from Stephen Mackreth's map of 1778, showing the area of the Fryerage, a private house of John Dalton occupying the site of the Dominican Friary. This 12-acre polygon of ground, the former Friary precinct, was soon to be developed on behalf of the Daltons as a desirable residential area. Lots were initially let out on 41-year leases.

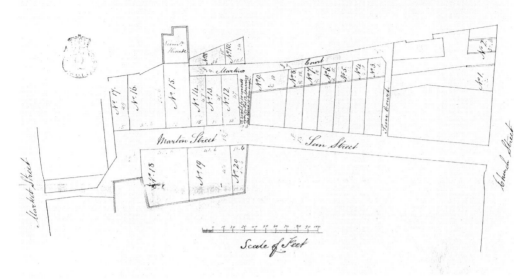

Plan of proposed building lots in Sun Street in 1797, occupying the former pleasure grounds of Rev. Oliver Marton, who died in 1794. The 'Summer House', hemmed in by lot 15, is today known as the 'Music Room'. Those lots not marked with numbers – to the right of the plan – had already been sold from the Molyneux estate in 1785. (Lancaster Central Library, MS4479)

The house itself was bought for £1,550 by Leonard Redmayne, Director of Gillows, the cabinet-makers, but since again few of the lots sold another auction took place in 1827.[89] In 1820 one of the lots on the corner of Cawthorne Street and High Street had been given as a site for the Girls' National School. Many of the buildings in this street have been replaced by yards and sheds for the Post Office but the Trades Hall and a pair of adjacent houses probably belong to the late 1820s or 1830s.

Among developments within the historic core only one calls for attention. Former pleasure grounds lying between China Lane and New Street, containing respectively a bowling green and the Music Room, were sold off from the Molyneux estates in 1785[90] and from the Marton estates in 1797[91] as building plots, producing what is now Sun Street. The Music Room, bereft of purpose, languished neglected and in decay behind industrial outbuildings until its restoration to its original splendour in 1976 by the Landmark Trust.[92]

Gazetteer of Georgian Buildings

BROCK STREET

No. 25
Part of the Dalton Square development and an integral part of the terrace on the western side, forming a unit with nos 11–12 Dalton Square, *q.v.*

CABLE STREET

Nos 1 and 3
Remains of a pair of houses by Richard Gillow *c.* 1759, with doors paired in centre. Six bays plus two extra bays at the side over a coach entrance × three storeys. Prominent keystones to windows, Doric columns to doorcases. Unusually for Lancaster the rear wing is of brick. The houses were built for Capt. Henry Fell and Mr Samuel Simpson.[93] At the rear of the houses is a former shared warehouse related to the old river course, divided in two by a lateral wall going right up to the apex of the roof. It has the date '1791' inscribed on a roof beam.

Cable Street, looking west *c.* 1925. The projecting railings or 'palisadoes' of nos 9 and 11, in the right foregound, are remarkably complete and show what has been lost elsewhere through road widening and wartime scrap drives.

Pen and wash drawing of the interior of Lancaster Castle in 1824 by James Weetman. On the left is the newly built Female Penitentiary while the arcade in the centre surrounds the twelfth-century Keep. Weetman drew this from a window in the 'Pin Box', in the rear of the Gatehouse. As this was one of the Debtors' rooms, he may well have been a debtor himself.

No. 5

House of five bays × three storeys. Centrally placed doorcase with Doric capitals.

Nos 9 and 11

Two houses of three bays each × three storeys with a basement, the two doorways centrally placed under one pediment with Doric capitals and approached by steps.

LANCASTER CASTLE

The great building programme between 1788 and 1823 included the Shire Hall, Crown Court, and Governor's house, designed by Thomas Harrison, and the Female Penitentiary and various other prison accommodation by Joseph Gandy.

The Shire Hall is a Gothick semi-polygonal structure with seven exterior faces, and a single Perpendicular window in each face. Behind it is the Crown Court, built against the outer face of the Lungess Tower, the medieval keep.

The Governor's House was fitted into the line of the former curtain wall between the gatehouse and the Well Tower. The whole of the northern side of the Castle was also demolished and subsequently extended, with new towers for prison accommodation, before 1807. Women prisoners were accommodated in a new range, the Female Penitentiary, one of the last major additions to the Castle, on the site of the medieval Dungeon Tower.[94] It is of interest to record the opinion of the Kent architect Daniel Alexander on the Shire Hall: '... The best [shire halls] are Stafford, York, Lancaster, and Chester ... Lancaster and Chester are very magnificent and beautiful structures (the former Gothic, the latter Greek) far surpassing any building we have in the south of England; but, sad to say, very bad to hear in ...'[95]

LANCASTER PRIORY CHURCH

West tower with pinnacles and pointed bell openings, designed by Henry Sephton of